In Love and Life

Esha Young

Matador
9 Priory Business Park
Kibworth Beauchamp
Leicestershire LE8 0RX, UK
Tel: (+44) 116 279 2299
Fax: (+44) 116 279 2277
Email: books@troubador.co.uk
Web: www.troubador.co.uk/matador

ISBN 978 1783060 795

British Library Cataloguing in Publication Data.
A catalogue record for this book is available from the British Library.

Printed and bound in the UK by TJ International, Padstow, Cornwall
Typeset in 11pt Adobe Garamond Pro by Troubador Publishing Ltd, Leicester, UK

Matador is an imprint of Troubador Publishing Ltd

FSC
www.fsc.org
MIX
Paper from responsible sources
FSC® C013056

In Love and Life

Scattered Ashes

Scattered ashes on the floor–
A sign that you were here;
The weakest link inside of me
invited your return.
A casual man for a casual girl
is what I should believe–
Encounters of this kind are not preferred.
The chimes above my door release their haunting lullaby,
The shadows in the hallway disappoint;
but whiskey in a glass–times two–can numb the careless edge,
lending purpose to the stranger at my wake.

Reminders

A favoured brand of lager with a complimentary stare–
A breakfast made of popsicles–
A crystal chandelier.
A morning where a butterfly bears witness to my wake–
A lantern made of paper–
A laughable mistake.
A near-forgotten photograph with colour fading fast–
A fountain made of chocolate–
A fishing line to cast.
A whisper at the picture-show where lovers congregate–
A traffic jam at midday–
An empty dinner plate.
The echo of a lonely dog howling at the moon–
A crashing wave against the rocks–
A black and white cartoon.
The thunderous clap of a stormy night knocking at my door–
A ladder to the attic–
Wet footprints on my floor.
Reminders of your every form dance inside my head
to a broken record in the dark–
Laughing in my bed.

Phantom Warrior

Shapes in the night and whispers from the trees
swirl around this phantom warrior;
transporting an illness to dimensions–brand new–
In a violent bid at ridicule.
Worthy chameleon, where are you now?
Negate all the madness–
The falsehood to bear;
Stumbles and bruises and sweat on the brow
are marks to be worn if the journey is fair;
and where songs ring out in the stillness of air,
a bubble will carry away what is there.
A pretty, plumed thing of the world calls out names
and tangles desires and delicate wounds;
Vixen and angel–
Volcano of flesh–
A kind without match at the end of the day;
sparingly offer, if bounty has failed
the crooked and weathered
with faces of shame.

Parasite

Strip me of this malady–
Run mercury through my veins;
Steal the truth at midnight
and whisk her far away.
Purge the script of history
and offer slates of new;
Bring mountains of crisp linens
and a pot of morning dew.
Make each new dream a sequence
that has never lived before
and idle hours trumpet with the tales of
something pure;
Give substance to this veil of sheer
to cast away the light–
Make sweet the land of living
for this thirsty parasite.

Destiny

They talk of meant-to-be–
Of destiny–
Of fate;
So many names for the timeless soul who keeps us hanging on.
A concept to cling to–
A fuel for night;
So many ways to romance the one who offers no easy answer.
A mind of her own–
State undefined;
Bank on the boons she dispenses;
A charming prospect–
Alluring and kind–
When cruel though, she can reject you.
So place your bets,
Take your chance,
Stir potions to nestle a fall;
Blind faith is naïve and falters at times,
Pray that she will not forget you.

Reflections

That summer of darkness still taunts me,
black shadows danced around my heart;
Sorrow found its beginning.

A perfect soul, a perfect smile,
the sweetest memories locked away;
Sorrow goes on living.

Questions raging through this fortress,
silence still the unkind beast;
Sorrow may be winning.

Five summers now, a new-born laugh,
that perfect smile renewed;
Sorrow leads to new beginnings.

Woman

The strength of her love is a mystery,
Her fortune smiles your way;
An icon in the pages of history,
A symbol of hope for today.
The hurt in your being will stir her,
The wars of the world steal her tears;
No cannons or guns can control her,
Faith is the armour she wears.
Fruit of the womb–
she gifts you–
A song on a thunderous day;
The passion of flesh to engage you–
An unconditional play.
No mirror can show her true beauty–
Some questions come rife with disdain–
A friend in the face of your jury;
A lover to take your name.

Peace

Your polished life of bounty
in a world of sheltered cares
is the nemesis of many,
where powers betray their fears.
No fault of yours–
this silver spoon–
No fault of theirs to yearn;
When fortune smiles,
we seize the day
and bask in its return.
Perhaps one day the gaps will bridge
and free will shall prevail;
Perhaps in time foundations fall
and peace shall come again.

Closure

Crashing against the torrents of life,
learning as I go;
A cynical world–
My fair-weather friend–
Is all I seem to know.
So sweet were my imaginings,
so tender was a touch;
The relic of a love so true dwells beneath the dust.
Forgotten words of anger resonate on their return,
Stolen chances linger like an ember as she burns;
To want the unattainable and perish with its doom
is the fate I share my days with in this cold, forsaken room.

Wanting

I cannot help but gaze upon the form of your soft lips,
Your utterings are music to my soul;
Silent longing in the shadows as I wait
for your embrace,
A look from you 'til then will make me whole.
Stealing glances,
moments broken
by commitments–
Ever there;
A wishing well of hope may last the night.
A diary of secrets with a bottle of my schemes;
Such weapons to betray in such a fight.

The Desert of Love

Flames caress my skin
as desire burns within,
yet a lingering kiss evades.
Amidst the empty squalor of fathomless pain
I long for a resting place.
I have travelled a distance but no welcomed end
has soothed my weary eye;
I feel my persistence now fading away
as the nomadic winds pass me by.
My parched lips have thirsted–
To taste of the new–
To know more than which I endure;
but my heart cannot believe
for it has been beaten by time
and the sands in the desert of love.

The Cage

The earth you tread, the air you breathe
are one and the same for me.
The world you see–
The masquerade–
Is my unwanted enemy.
Desperate to share the truth inside–
The one that no one knows–
The anchor of my solitude is fear I will not show.
All the laughing faces swimming in the crowd,
All the fallen whispers once again call to me now;
An open mind is all I seek to yield an open heart,
Freedom is the impetus from which I will not part.
The vision of a life complete, is mine, as it is yours;
The essence of a good man must lie mingled with his flaws;
If we should one day meet as equals in this pantomime–
stripped bare–
My struggle will reveal itself through a conscience–ever clear.

Troubled Hand

Troubled hand against my shoulder,
you find me once again;
the game of solitaire is at an end.
You took the crooked highway–
A path we could not share–
A victim of confusion–
You pretend.

There were no tears of waiting
or raging war within;
the tide of life rolls on from day to day.
You chose the road most travelled
but did not realize
a pair of wings can turn the other way.

Some gifts we take for granted–
In ignorance we stand–
Human nature never lets us down.
Weathered eyes now gaze upon me–
A look I knew would come–
The words they speak were never more profound.

Darkness

Why smile at their misfortune
and celebrate their tears?
No bitter hand can justify contempt.
A disregard for broken men is all you can conceive–
Such hollow rations spare you no expense.
Be this a failing or a conquest–
in such unravelling, woeful times–
To ridicule at will for game or sport?
Unveil your wise philosopher–
unmask the pages read–
With disrepute,
I meet your school of thought.

Emotional Devoid

Speak the words I want to hear but let them all be true–
Sweet nothings are a poison to me now;
The untrained eye will praise your flaws and revel in disgrace–
Once bitten, twice as strong am I somehow.

No mourning shall deliver me where victims find retreat–
A callous mind deserves no bleeding heart;
No struggle shall accompany the wake of my release–
Deception is a shallow work of art.

So wander through the streets of your emotional devoid–
Make peace with blinding lights and empty stares;
The enigma of your solitude is deadly in its charm–
Evasive as your complementary pair.

Gabriel

Fate in all her beauty has bewitched me–
A beacon of perfection is bestowed–
A wispy cloud has swept me up into the fairest skies
with my heart upon my sleeve for all to know.
A dream was in the making–
Some thought it fantasy–
The echo of his laughter is my own;
A piece of me–
The dawn of love–
Unending as surreal–
No boundaries or conditions to behold.
A maiden in this voyage of euphoria,
The angel of my being now descends;
Reaching forth to wrap my grateful arms around him,
In love and life, creation never ends.

A Love Apart

As tales unfold–and memories made–with a promise I depart,
The raptures of your melody will warm my heavy heart;
Lonely days will pass me by with musings of your smile,
A sanctuary to bury me, if only for a while.
So I carry with me burdens of a troubled hour,
avoiding darkness in its cruel bid to consume with all its
power;
The miles between are not as cold or of the bitter kind,
Patience brings a rendezvous–
much more than some may find.
Weeping willows melt into the pathway of this home
where a constant love is burning in the cauldron of my soul.

Euphoric

Wonders of a love surround me
and purpose is revealed;
Hush the hustling, hurried world
and all uncertainties I feel.
No absence of mind shall fill my days–
Or lukewarm tenderness–
A nurturing of tiny hands
will bring togetherness.
This treasure in its grace astounds me
and shelters me from pain;
with every breath of being–
In belief of strength sustained.
I smile upon this four leaf clover
dancing at my door;
Such joy in its simplicity
can leave you wanting more…

Breaking the Chain

The wild wind carries with it pieces of a fateful day,
The splintered hands of bondage breathe a sigh;
This winter morning stirs–
as did the one which came before–
Tomorrow will forget the tears you cried.
Fragile and alone in such adversity–
But strong enough–
In anguish you survived;
The steps you take will lead a generation,
Your triumph keeps maternal dreams alive.

Spoils of War

He stands among the rubble
drowned in lifeless pools of blue–
I do not hear his voice or know his name;
With mountains and a lifetime in between us–
I cannot feel the measure of his pain.
The chaos of injustice has bled his tender years–
A wonderment at peace can breed contempt;
A vicious circle preys among the talent of his kind–
A haunted slumber just will not relent.
If the inhumane could spare us–
as we choose or as we need–
Life could then be made of better things;
but his playground is a graveyard–
and with broken dreams to mend–
This innocent,
on the hangman's noose,
he swings.

Sacrifices

Do not love me if you have to
but love me if you care;
A halfway heart is nothing–
And anything but fair.
It will hurt to watch you leave,
Even more to watch you stay;
The truth can cut in places new
as mercy falls away.
Convention says you tarry–
Convention can be cruel–
The agony of love gone cold
can render you a fool.
So with my blessing take your leave
and find your wings again;
A chance at love unscathed,
Another chapter to begin.

Hope

I come to you in times of strife
or utter disbelief;
Please call on me to face the worst
when brought down on your knees.
A loyal friend to many,
yet some forget my name;
A saving grace to hold your hand
but powerless to fate.
Some love me when the skies are blue
but curse me when it rains;
A friend indeed is always there through laughter and the pain.
My smile will never falter,
My face will stay the same;
Think of me in times of need,
Do not forget my name.

Conjured Circumstance

I wear the mask of anger to shelter tears that fall–
Weakness is a failing you exploit–
Worthy lovers kiss your wounds and breathe your salty air
but I can hear the laughter in your voice.
So I shut the door behind me
pondering this ache,
We see the silver lining in romance;
A fool but once and never more to stumble on that place–
A victim of my conjured circumstance.

Release

The hollow of time and these blasphemous hours
are like spokes of a wheel near-forgotten;
Thunder and lightning fail to ignite–
The curious remain indisposed.
Rapturous guilt in a mingling of worlds–
A place where old conflicts arise;
A patient man–with his fleeting thoughts–
Is certainly bound to explode.
Rifling through pages of words never spoken,
adrift on the clouds of a cumbersome day;
Waiting in vain for a fortune once promised
in a casual glance once given away.
With a crash and a bang–
And a cry in the dark–
Cutting through panes–spilling sand on the floor–
A quivering hand reaches out to console him–
A carnal angel of torment no more.

Sudden Traveller

In the dead of night this traveller roams–hunted and betrayed–
Hungry for a morning free of whispers from behind;
The echo of contemptuous laughter rips right through her veins,
a shadow of doubt in the mire of lies cannot free her from the stain.
Judgemental eyes–in a world of vice–seem bent on her demise,
free thinkers dare not conjure lives unfit for compromise;
Straightjackets and caricatures are choices much preferred,
a chartered course is set in stone and nothing shall defer;
Make such lines invisible and suffer every turn,
in the wake of freedom comes a caution–some cannot discern.
In the dead of night this traveller dreams in a bed now made for one,
shedding the tepid smile conceived to temper everyone.

Come

Running through fragmented pockets
counting shadows before the break–
A tunnel of tranquillity is waiting up ahead.
Sometimes old and some things new
breathe life into this home
that hints of moments washed away and blistered by the storm.
Casting doubt upon fair chances seems the error of all ways
and feasts upon the thirsty flesh with calculated haste;
Deeds flow freely from expression–in excess of what is known–
And blind the naked eye that dares to look beyond the shade.
A companion for the hungry days of wanton recklessness
may not provide the easiest of answers in these times;
but lonely tears and lonely ways fester in the night
where the palest maidens bring release if called in from the
light.

Dissolution

Lie with me–
Not to me–
Lock the door before you dial;
Return with arms wide open
and that pretty, painted smile.

Voices may recede;
Bodies can be cold;
Until the moment comes to go
I might just need a thought to hold.

The fading shimmer that was ours
may leave with much ado,
and tatters of this ivory dress will claim the place of someone new;
No crystal ball or magic cards lend portraits of the rain,
A thing is known–
But still unknown–
And never is the same.

Mismatched

Please understand this silence in your colour-coated world–
The failure of expression means no shortage of desire;
Your feathered wings can hover over land and sea alike–
I stumble in my reach to quell the ache of this divide.
Like fireflies to the one light,
they come forth in swollen droves;
This dark and heavy corner gives retreat
and food for thought;
Watching from this perch and sketching victories of my own,
There is no chair for cowardice in the court that holds your
throne.
Faint-hearted may surrender to the realm of fantasy
where possession is just as sweet a thing;
Faint-hearted may play witness to another dream fulfilled
and never come to grasp the binding ring.

Lost Love

She rocked the boat and shelter with a petulant refrain
and drew the breath of vermin in his stare;
Retraction and reflection did not melt the frosty wall
that found a fuel in her permanent despair.
The swan of tender youth had met the coldest winter yet,
The looking glass of shame refused to break;
Abundant in her offerings of penance and recourse–
Deaf ears to match a cruel turn of fate.
A pocketbook of pictures rests beside a half-filled bed
and caters to his solitary hand;
The poison of a spoken word can echo for all time
and drown the fallen angel under footprints in the sand.

Treasure

Tiny treasures in the sand
and surf at my feet;
A kiss of sun on golden skin–
A customary treat.
The taste of valour fills me up
and decorates the shore;
This charming realm of ecstasy has left me wanting more.
Insatiable desire and salvation–once unknown–
Now take me to the brink of sheer delight;
I lift my eyes up to the skies
and with a sultry breath,
I drink the moment of this candour,
counting shooting stars at night.

Last fall

Fists of water pound at your chest
and mutant names revolve;
A crooked, half-baked cigarette
is lying on the floor.
A gentle breeze surrounds this fire–
fanning at the flame–
A mortal wound is none at all
if partnered with this game.
Languid pools of amber mirrors
mocking every glare,
Listening to imaginary sounds;
A lamb in darkness–
earning stripes in accusations lain–
takes no pleasure in the trials that abound.
Pools run dry and speeches wane
and scratching paws recede;
A back is turned and fades away
to anonymity.

Material Things

Pennies and trifles–and things to give up–
Leave the trail of an infertile shell;
Musings and gestures and things to exalt
are all patrons of personal hell.
Sheets of paper and permanent ink
do not conjure a thought on their own;
If I could supply the simplest of facts,
may these demons become overthrown.
To confess is to feel
perhaps mercy or gain
or the leisure of pastures of green.
To deny is to live
in the shadows of love
where passion can never be free.

Growing Up –
An individual journey

Sixteen–a master of doubt and reserve–
holds a fistful of colours in a pocket of woes–
Carving a person on the edge of a shore–
Gangly arms, fingers and toes.
Twenty brings will and a taste of the world–
just enough to mislead with a know-it-all smile–
Designing an idol for leads of a page–
Effortless charm–mighty and wise.
A quartered century holds secrets and truths
that infallible ones gather close to the chest;
Reshaping ideas of a rickety past,
Planting new seeds without haste or regret.
Three tens mean certainty of self and desire
without fear to relinquish the needs once withheld–
Sharing the best of a character flaw–
weakness and strength–nothing misread.
Two twenties–the ego has countered some blows–
Surviving despite a few delicate scars–
Content with the bounty–inside and out–
No hunt for a fountain of youth or fast cars.

Carousel

A carousel grinds to a maddening halt,
Two patrons alight with wandering stares;
Hands do not touch and voices recoil
and tickets go separate ways.
Sugar-topped treats and candy of cotton–
Gone sour and tossed to the side–
Is all that is left of this leisure parade
and all its adventurous rides.
Prizes once won and spare tokens retained
gather quick dust in a room;
Musical boxes and pictures for two
grace the soundtrack of romantic doom.

Black and White

The trickle at my feet can drown this love,
A speckle of disdain from you can melt these sturdy walls;
Comparisons and alleged flaws sit idly in this home
where foundations grow as easy as they fall.
I came to you so long ago–with nothing much to give–
You drew me to your arms without a care;
Incessant stings of gratitude now leave these salty lips
where the taste of someone else still lingers there.
Illusions have been shattered and reality remains–
Is anything enough to keep us bound?
The black and white–and shades of grey–have mingled with the night
and call upon my name to save us now.
Distance and a longing might prevail when lovers break–
If this is strong, then somehow it shall heal;
I take the road that brought me here and tell you as I go–
This heart of mine is always yours to steal.

Ties that Bind

Dances with puppets and dinners of bones
fill this chamber of tiresome feet;
the jack of all trades sings a silent refrain
for the queen of the savoury and sweet.
Standing alone on the edge of the floor–
casting looks that could tame a shrew–
Is a knight of the order of pride and conceit
in a pair of imaginary shoes.
Bags full of coins and favourite things
swim in melting pots of a brew
made of bits of this and samples of that
and gallons of things never knew.
Daggers, spears and armour of words
keep their place at the iron-cast gate;
Vacant shapes and luminous sneers meander
through compounded waste.
A timeless abyss where penance is null–
and the cost of return is forfeit–
Hosts the skeletal romance with goods in excess–
The bargain made under these streets.

Inequality

They talk of modernity–
New age and the times–
Yet the youngest of victims are sisters of mine;
Cut off from the choices that I freely make–
Instructed–
Abducted–
Enslaved–
And betrayed.
Stand up–they may die–like many before
who braved conditions that bind;
Bonds lead the way–
If of the right kind–
So sisters, reside in one mind.
The primitive laws made by those at the helm
must melt with the union of hearts;
The path is not easy when power is prize–
Evolution takes patience and time.
But when the time comes–blood might be spilled–
The mighty may not fall so fast;
A tireless fight for a civilized place
may banish tyrannical past.

Non-Fiction

This is no make-believe–no subtle shift of thought–
This is no substitute for love or something of the sort.
This is a weary girl–a made-up, laughing face–
A sample of non-fiction in a solitary place.
This can be many things–when considered for its parts–
But nothing like a severed tie can take me to the start.
Admission gives the healing that life summons from our
wounds,
Confessions of disjointed limbs supply the antidote;
A rendezvous of answers lies wide awake somewhere,
with one mysterious morning–
In want of repair.

Chances

A fickle lover leaves–
Your well runs dry once more;
You hide behind the masquerade–
Ignore the knock upon your door;
So tender is the hope that lingers in this sound,
longing for a turn to show its worth.
A doubtful mind recedes,
playing games you never win;
If chance meets fate or circumstance,
love can breathe again.

Whisper of a Breeze

In the whisper of a breeze
or song of the dawn;
with the dewdrops on the trees,
time hurries along
and escapes us.
Provoked by nothing–
Sometimes–
Chasing mortal dreams,
forgetting what it means
to love–
To trust–
To give–
To lust
for the comfort of a day
without the setting sun
casting shadows over beating hearts
and wounded men.
Remember how to feel–
To yield the slightest touch–
In the whisper of a breeze
life can be gone.